JUNIOR PET CARE

RABBITS

ZUZA VRBOVA

Photography Susan Miller
Art Robert McAulay
With additional photos by Vincent Serbin

Reading and Child Psychology Consultant
Dr. David Lewis

ACKNOWLEDGMENTS

With special thanks to Mrs. Evans, Headmistress,
and the children of Havers Infants School,
Also to David Collier, DTP advisor;
DECODE DESIGN, Jenny Toft at PET BOWL,
Mr. Hollingsworth, Rabbit Breeder,
Andrew Menzies, Menor Photographic Services.

Junior Pet Care

Guinea Pigs
Hamsters
Kittens
Parakeets
Puppies
Rabbits
Snakes
Turtles

This edition © 1998 Chelsea House Publishers, a division of Main Line Book Company.

1 3 5 7 9 8 6 4 2

Library of Congress Cataloging-in-Publication Data applied for

ISBN 0-7910-4904-3

CIP

CONTENTS

NOTE TO PARENTS

Having a pet plays an important part in growing up and rabbits make ideal pets because they are very responsive and tame. **RABBITS** portrays the fun of rabbit keeping. It gives a glimpse of the priceless pleasure that children gain from caring for and playing with their rabbit. At the same time it provides the vital information that both the parent and child need to be able to enjoy their rabbit to the fullest. The book has been specially written in consultation with Dr. David Lewis, a leading specialist in child development. He has written numerous books on the subject of child psychology. **RABBITS** benefits greatly from his wide experience in successfully motivating and understanding children with a diversity of background and age.

YOU AND YOUR RABBIT

Rabbits are quiet, furry animals. If you take care of your rabbit well, you will have a loyal and affectionate pet in return. It is important to always be kind and gentle to your rabbit. You should cuddle and stroke it often.

Remember, a rabbit is not a toy but a real living animal. Once you have bought a rabbit, you will have to look after it for a long time. You will have to provide food and water and clean the hutch.

Making sure that your rabbit always has a cozy bed and plenty to eat is part of the fun of owning a pet. It is a bit like having a new baby. Your rabbit will be completely dependent on you.

THE TIME OF YEAR TO BUY A RABBIT

Spring is a good time to buy a rabbit. The pleasant spring days followed by the warm summer and then fall will give you plenty of time to learn about rabbit keeping and to enjoy being outdoors with your new pet. It takes time and patience to learn all about your rabbit, but rabbit keeping can become an interesting hobby you can enjoy all your life.

Take good care of your rabbit and you will have its friendship for years to come.

CHOOSING YOUR RABBIT

A female rabbit *is called a* **doe** *and a male rabbit is called a* **buck.** *They both make lovely pets. If you think that you might be allowed to* *let your rabbit have babies in the future then it is a good idea for you to buy a doe right from the start.*

Rabbits come in several colors and sizes and with different kinds of coats. You can buy giant rabbits or miniature rabbits. Some have long fluffy fur and others have sleek velvety coats. Some are white, some are black, brown or patterned—with brown ears and a white body, for example.

DIFFERENT KINDS OF RABBIT

If you want a special kind of rabbit, you might need to buy one that belongs to a particular **breed.** This

Dutch rabbits *weight about 5 lbs (2kg) when they are grown up. In a good example of the breed, the white fur behind the neck extends clear to the waist.*

There are several breeds of lop rabbit, all of which have ears that hang down. Lop rabbits should never be handled by their ears.

means that the rabbit you choose will have some distinctive characteristics. For example, the Flemish Giant breed is always a big rabbit that weighs about 4 lbs (6.3 kg), has a pleasant nature, large ears and thick fur. On the other hand, the Netherland Dwarf breed is a very little rabbit that comes in a variety of colors and only weights just over 2 lbs. (2 kg). The Polish is another small rabbit—a thinner version of the Netherland Dwarf—and tends to have a more fiery temper.

There are more than 50 breeds for you to choose from.

Buying a rabbit from a pet store.

CROSS-BRED RABBITS

The rabbits you see in a pet store are sometimes mixtures of breeds, rather than being of one breed. These are **cross-bred** rabbits, with a mother and father of different breeds.

Because cross-bred rabbits are a mixture of breeds you cannot predict how big they will grow to be or what their personalities will be like when they are fully grown rabbits.

Cross-bred rabbits are not as costly as some rabbits of particular breeds nor as valuable because their coloring and size vary so greatly. Nevertheless, they make excellent and rewarding pets.

Choosing a rabbit is fun, especially since there are so many breeds from which you can choose.

Some people feel that smaller rabbits are easier for children to handle, but if you prefer big rabbits there is really no reason why you should not have one. However you must have enough room for a large rabbit.

Rabbits need plenty of room to play in, and a big rabbit would be very uncomfortable hunched up in a small cage. Imagine what you would feel like if you did not have enough space to stretch and play in your bedroom. So, if you have only a small amount of space to keep your rabbit in, and have only a small hutch, it is important to buy a small breed like the Netherland Dwarf.

A blue Himalayan rabbit. She is two years old and 15 ins. (36 cm) long.

THE AGE OF YOUR RABBIT

It is best to buy a baby rabbit because once a rabbit has settled into a new home it does not like to be moved about. Grown-up rabbits that are moved sometimes refuse to eat or act strangely at first to show they are upset. Make sure that your new baby rabbit is at least 6 weeks old. A rabbit that is any younger than this is too young to be separated from its mother.

A 6-week old Netherland Dwarf rabbit, ready to go to a new home.

A HOME FOR YOUR RABBIT

Before you buy your rabbit it is important for you to have everything ready first. Then, when you arrive home with your new pet, you can settle it into its comfortable new hutch.

RABBIT WARRENS

In the wild, rabbits live in a **warren.** This is a network of tunnels they dig out under the ground. The young are born in a nest which the mother makes out of grass or moss. She lines it with fur pulled from her own body. Although lots of rabbits live together in a rabbit warren, they each have

their own separate tunnel area. That
is why pet rabbits prefer to live on
their own or with just one other
rabbit.

Pet rabbits are kept in hutches. A hutch is simply a cozy cage or container, usually made of wood with a wire front so the rabbit can see what is going on outside.

The bigger the hutch you can provide, the better it will be for your rabbit. Just like you, rabbits prefer to run around rather than being cooped up in a confined space. Also, rabbits like to sit up sometimes, and the ceiling of the hutch needs to be high enough for the rabbit to be able to sit up comfortably.

Because rabbits are shy animals, they like to be able to hide at times and so prefer their hutch to be divided into two compartments, much like a bedroom and a living room.

This hutch is designed so the front can be removed completely, which makes it easier to clean.

A piece of wood helps to keep the rabbit's bedding from spilling out of the hutch. It can be taken out to make cleaning the hutch a simple job.

KEEPING YOUR RABBIT OUTDOORS

Once you have made or bought your rabbit's hutch, you must decide where you are going to keep the hutch.

Hutches can be indoor or outdoor homes. Rabbits do not mind being housed outside all year round as long as the hutch is in a sheltered spot, protected from the wind. It is best to put your outdoor hutch on an old table so that you can easily reach inside to take care of your rabbit.

A hutch with legs makes it easier for you to feed and clean your rabbit.

AN INDOOR HUTCH

You can keep your rabbit indoors as long as the room is not stuffy and there is enough light. Rabbits like and need to have plenty of fresh air. A shed or an unused garage is a good place for an indoor hutch.

STRAW traps air and will keep the rabbit warm at night.

HAY can also be clipped to the outside of the cage in a wire hay rack so that your rabbit can have clean hay to eat whenever it wants.

An indoor hutch which opens up like a lid to a box. It is kept in a school and the children help to care for the rabbit.

MAKING THE RABBIT'S BED

A rabbit will not feel comfortable sleeping on the bare wooden floorboards of the hutch and needs some absorbent material to make a bed with. There are several different kinds of material, called **litter,** that you can use for making your rabbit's hutch comfortable, especially during cold winter nights. You can line the hutch with newspaper.

Hay is one of the best kinds of litter. You can also use sawdust, dry peat, fallen leaves or straw. Whatever kind of litter you use, it must be changed once or twice every week.

All rabbits like exercise and they enjoy being allowed to run about freely. To make sure that your rabbit is safe while it is outside exploring your garden, it is best to make an enclosed area especially for the rabbit. This is called a rabbit run.

A run is a simple structure made of a wooden frame with wire netting on all sides. You can take your rabbit out gently from the hutch where it sleeps every night and carry it to the garden run. Here your rabbit will be away from any cats and dogs that could harm it, and your parents' favorite plants will be safe from being eaten, by your pet. Also, by having a

A Morant hutch is a triangular cage with a wire floor. It can be moved about the lawn every few days so that your rabbit can munch on fresh new grass.

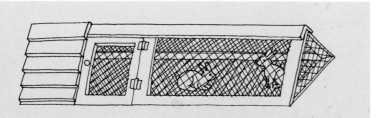

run you will avoid having to chase your bunny all around the garden when it is time to put it back in the hutch. Never leave your rabbit out in the sun for long in the summer. Rabbits have thick fur coats that keep them very warm and rabbits can die very quickly from too much sun if they cannot find any shade. Always be sure that your pet has plenty to drink when it is in the run.

OTHER EQUIPMENT

Besides the hutch you will need a feeding container and a water bottle. You can buy these at most pet stores.

Enjoying a fresh spring day in a rabbit run can be more fun for a rabbit than being in a hutch.

TAKING YOUR RABBIT
HOME

As a general rule look for the rabbit which is most lively. Your rabbit should also have a well-rounded, firm body. An active youngster that you can see hopping about with the rest of the rabbit family is likely to be healthier than one which sits quietly in a corner on its own when you approach it. Check to see if the ears twitch in response to different sounds—like you clapping.

To help keep your rabbit healthy, its hutch will have to be cleaned out regularly. This is like changing your bedclothes and washing the sheets—your rabbit will certainly appreciate having a clean hutch.

When you think you have found the rabbit you want, you need to look at it very carefully to make sure it is healthy before you buy it. There are several things that you will need to consider.

The eyes should be bright.

The nose should be dry. Never buy a rabbit with

a runny nose, as this can be sign of a serious illness.

The coat should be sleek or, if the rabbit is a baby, it may be nice and fluffy. Check that the fur is not dirty around the tail, as this is often a sign of a stomach upset.

The ears should be clean inside. If there are brown scabs here the rabbit might have ear mites.

Ask the owner what the rabbit has been used to eating. You should then provide the same food as the rabbit's previous owner at about the same times during the first few days. This will help your new pet to settle into its new home, as at least part of its routine will remain the same. Later you can slowly change to your own preferred food and feeding times. After a few days try to give your new rabbit half of its usual type of food and half of the new kind of food.

Giving new foods gradually will mean the rabbit's stomach can become accustomed to these changes slowly.

Besides being away from its mother and brothers and sisters for the first time, the young rabbit will have to adjust to strange surroundings and different people with new voices.

Take a safe basket or box when you go to buy your rabbit. It could be frightening for your rabbit to be carried about without knowing exactly where it is going. Rabbits that are frightened will struggle and try to escape. They could hurt themselves if their container cannot be closed properly. When you arrive home with your new rabbit, place it straight into the hutch that you have already prepared.

When you take your new rabbit out of his carrier, he may be nervous. Handle him gently and carefully.

FEEDING

At supper time, this rabbit eagerly waits to see his owner.

Rabbits like a regular routine so you should feed them at the same time every day. Within a few days you will find your rabbit eagerly waiting for you at the front of the hutch at feeding time. It will be watching and listening for you to come with some food.

You can buy special pots for your rabbit's food in pet stores. These are heavier than a regular saucer or plate, so the rabbit cannot tip its food over easily. There are also several styles of water bottle to choose from.

Rabbits are **herbivores.** This means that they do not eat meat. But, just like you, they need different kinds of food and they appreciate a variety. But of course, they do not like sudden changes with completely new foods.

The best food for your rabbit is rabbit pellets. Pellets should be the main diet of pet rabbits, with other foods offered only once in a while as special treats.

Pellets are ready-made food for the rabbit that you can buy from the pet store. They contain everything the rabbit needs to keep healthy and fit. They are a complete meal.

Some rabbits like bread or bran soaked in a little milk and water, especially in winter. Make this fresh every day. But most rabbits prefer dry, crisp foods rather than wet, sloppy, dishes. The dry foods also help to keep their teeth in trim, so they do not grow too long. Unlike your front teeth, those of a rabbit will continue growing all its life.

Rabbit mix is another alternative which you can buy from the pet store. Rabbit mix contains a mixture of cereals such as crushed oats, maize and barley. It is a bit more interesting than pellets, and rabbits enjoy it. You can mix this with their pellets. Be sure this food is always kept dry.

Whatever you feed your rabbit, you can also always include hay. This is because it contains **fiber,** which is essential for the well-being

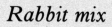

Rabbit mix

Rabbit pellets

Rabbit cake

Rabbit treats

of your rabbit. Hay also keeps rabbits from being bored, and they usually like to have a nibble of some hay during the day. The hay can either be loose in the hutch or on a hay rack.

The best hay has been kept for a few months, but it should still smell fresh and contain wild plants. Check to make sure that it isn't moldy or dirty. Try to avoid giving your rabbit any very fresh, newly baled hay, be-

Cauliflower

Carrots

cause this sometimes gives your rabbit a stomach problem.

The kinds of food that rabbits like which your family might leave are stale dry bread and green food such as the outside leaves of lettuces and cabbages as well as apple and carrot peel that otherwise might just be thrown away.

Rabbits also like fresh plants, especially weeds which could be growing in your garden or in your neighborhood. But don't give your rabbit too much green food such as grass, clover and dandelions. Too much green food can make your rab-

Cabbage

Lettuce

Celery

bit ill. Also, make sure that all the fresh green food you use for your rabbit has been washed and check that no chemicals or insecticides have been near it. Never give your rabbit dirty wild leaves, bulbs from the garden, rhubarb, uncooked potato peel or tomato leaves, as these are poisonous.

Most people feed their rabbits at a certain time in the morning and evening, just as you have breakfast and supper. You might decide to feed your rabbit with a cupful of rabbit pellets and hay in the morning. The

pellets can be supplemented by rabbit mix, bread and raw vegetables in the evening.

The best way to judge how much food to give is to watch your rabbit. A well-fed rabbit should look eager for its food but will leave a few pellets or lettuce leaves in the feeding pot until perhaps the time for the following meal.

If you can manage to feed your rabbit only once a day, it is best to give him supper rather than breakfast, because rabbits often eat more in the evening than during the day.

Thistle

Plantain

Cow parsley

LOOKING AFTER
YOUR RABBIT

The more you take your rabbit out of its hutch, the tamer it will become. Rabbits that are not often taken out of their hutch are most likely to struggle or scratch. This is because they feel insecure. They can sense they might be dropped. Learn to handle your rabbit gently and firmly from the start so it can become used to you.

From the moment you open the hutch door your movements should be deliberate, slow and quiet. Rabbits

Learning to hold a rabbit.

are frightened of jerky movements and sudden noises. They remember if they have been handled roughly, and this might make them shy of people. You can tell if this has happened to a rabbit before because it cowers at the back of the hutch when the door is opened until it is left alone again. Once a rabbit has lost confidence in being handled by a child or a grown-up, it is difficult to get it to trust an owner again. So it is very important for you to learn how to hold your bunny safely and correctly. The easiest way for you to hold your rabbit is to place one hand under its body and the other around the head and ears, keeping the rabbit against your chest but not near your face. Try and relax when you are doing this for the first time, otherwise you might hold the rabbit's head too tightly and hurt it. Ask a grown-up to show you and help you at first.

Never pick a rabbit up by its ears or the scruff of its neck. You might see an experienced rabbit owner put a hand on the rabbit's ears, but this is only to steady and calm the rabbit.

It is easiest to take your rabbit out of the hutch backwards. This way you are less likely to be scratched and your rabbit's legs are less likely to catch on the door.

Support the body of the rabbit when you hold it.

TRIMMING THE CLAWS

The claws of a wild rabbit wear down naturally, but pet rabbits need their claws trimmed every so often because they are in a hutch for much of the time. Ask a grown-up to help you to do this with claw clippers. For a small rabbit you can use an ordinary pair of nail clippers.

TALKING TO YOUR RABBIT

Chat with your rabbit while you are taking care of it so that it will get to know you and not be afraid of your voice.

A rabbit's claws being clipped (below left).

Special rabbit claw clippers (below).

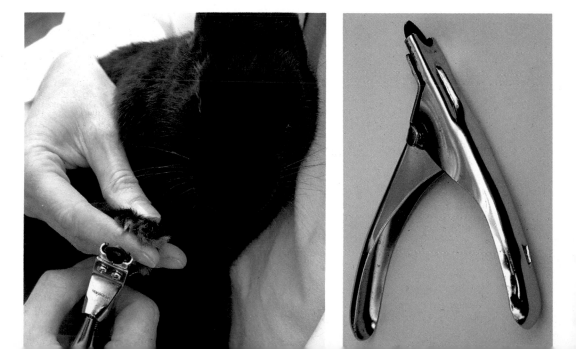

An affectionate rabbit

Rabbits are normally quiet animals, but they sometimes make a screaming noise if they see one of their natural enemies, like a dog or a cat, or even a larger and stronger rabbit. As you get to know your rabbit you will notice that it makes tiny sounds.

These are the little soft grunts and broken purrs that baby rabbits make when they talk to their mothers. If you are quiet and listen carefully you might hear these noises.

Grown-up rabbits may thump their back legs to talk to each other at

a distance. If one rabbit thumps, all the others will stop eating or running about and become still. This is one of their danger signals. Sometimes one thump is answered by another thump from another rabbit.

Stroking and combing your rabbit helps the coat to look shiny and healthy.

MOLTING

Rabbits lose their first baby coat of fur when they are about four months old. The adult fur has been gradually growing underneath. Rabbits, like lots of other animals, shed their coat of fur and grow a new one every year.

HEALTH CARE

If you keep your rabbit clean and well fed it should have a long and healthy life. Rabbits sometimes live for about 10 to 15 years—which means owning a rabbit is a long-term commitment for you.

In the same way as you might catch a cold or have a tummy upset, there are some common illnesses that rabbits might suffer from. Look at your rabbit carefully every day to make sure that it is healthy.

If your rabbit looks unhappy, sitting glumly in the corner of the hutch, with no appetite, or has a runny nose and eyes or loose droppings, it is probably not a well rabbit. If you think your rabbit is ill, ask a grown-up to help you take it to a veterinarian.

VACCINATING YOUR RABBIT

Depending where you live, you may be able to have your rabbit vaccinated against a disease called myxomatosis. It is caused by a virus that is spread from one wild rabbit to another by fleas. Wild rabbits may infect your pet.

The vet is giving this pet rabbit an injection to protect it from disease.

The vaccine to protect rabbits from this disease is not available everywhere.

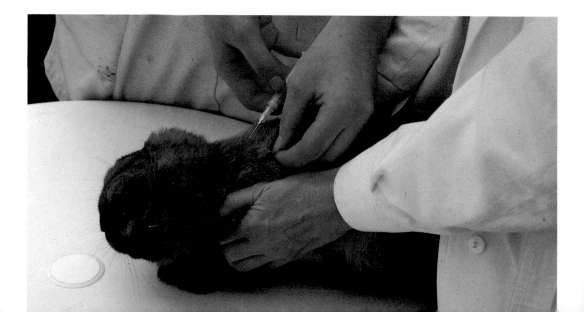

Cleaning the hutch is much easier if you do it often—at least once a week. The golden rule about when to clean your rabbit's hutch is a simple one. If you can smell a rabbit hutch it needs cleaning. This is especially important because flies may be attracted to the hutch and could harm your rabbit.

Cleaning the hutch is simple if you put several layers of newspaper on the floor of the hutch before you put your rabbit's mattress of straw or hay in. Then all you need to do is to pick up the newspaper with all the soiled bedding and throw it away and start again.

Some rabbits are tidy and leave their droppings in one corner of the

This rabbit has hurt its toe. The best thing to do is simply put antiseptic cream on the sore part. If the rabbit has a minor injury like this, avoid handling it too much for a few days.

hutch. If you have a rabbit like this, you can put a small tray of sawdust in the corner and your rabbit will learn to use it. All you have to do is remove the tray and refill it with fresh sawdust each day.

Every month or so, especially during the summer, the whole hutch should have a big, proper clean. You can scrub it out using water and then leave it to dry in the sun. This is like changing your bedlinens and washing the sheets. Keeping the hutch thoroughly clean like this will help to keep your rabbit healthy. Your rabbit will certainly appreciate having a nice clean hutch to live in. Be sure that the doors are always closed properly so that it cannot escape.

Rabbits can jump out of your arms, as this one did— hurting its front tooth on the hutch door in the process.

Some Common Rabbit Ailments

Diarrhea
Young rabbits are most likely to have tummy upsets. Just like babies, their tummies are very delicate and sensitive to new or sour food. If you notice your young rabbit looking unhappy, sitting huddled up in the corner of the hutch, and if it has loose, soft droppings it might have a tummy upset. There is often nothing that can be done. Remove any food that might have caused the trouble. You could also try feeding strawberry, bramble, raspberry or shepherd's purse leaves because often a rabbit is tempted to eat these if it is off its normal food.

Coccidiosis
This is caused by tiny creatures, called coccidia, which may be found in a rabbit's stomach. These may make a rabbit lose weight although it may continue to eat well. The coat loses its shine and the rabbit may also have loose droppings. The disease may be cured by a drug from the veterinarian or by feeding the rabbit with pellets that contain the drug, called coccidostats.

Sores
It is important to look at the base of your rabbit's legs regularly. They should have a thick coating of fur here. Some rabbits, especially Rex breeds, have very thin fur here, and it sometimes gets worn away, causing painful sore patches. This does not often happen with pet rabbits because it is usually caused by a rabbit's being kept in cages with wire floors. The cure is to keep the rabbit on a thick pile of bedding and put some zinc cream on the sore patch until it heals. Dirty, wet bedding can result in a similar problem.

Malocclusion of teeth
Normally a rabbit's upper and lower front teeth touch as the rabbit eats. Sometimes the teeth do not meet and carry on growing until the rabbit cannot eat at all. There is no real cure for this unfortunate condition, apart from cutting them back regularly. A veterinarian will do this for you.

PNEUMONIA

This is an inflammation of the lungs and often results from the rabbit being in a draft or in damp conditions. With pneumonia, the rabbit's breathing becomes very rapid. The rabbit will look miserable. It huddles up and loses its appetite. The best thing to do is keep the rabbit warm, with plenty of bedding and plenty of fresh air. Medicine from your veterinarian may help, but it is a serious illness, and should be prevented.

SNUFFLES

This is a disease that begins with the rabbit sneezing a lot. At first it might seem as though the sneezing is caused simply by dusty bedding, but if it continues and the rabbit also has a runny nose, then it is best to take the rabbit to a veterinarian, who will probably prescribe antibiotic medicine for your pet.

CANKER

This is caused by a small ear mite. If the rabbit is suffering from canker it will constantly shake its head and scratch its ears with its hind legs. It will also have yellowy-brown lumps in its ear. Never try to clean the rabbit's ear. You can buy ear drops for your rabbit from a pet store. Part of the treatment is cleaning out the rabbit hutch to make sure there are no more ear mites to re-infect your rabbit.

Glossary

Buck A male rabbit.

Cross-bred A rabbit is called a cross-bred when its parents are each a different breed.

Doe A female rabbit.

Fiber An important nutrient for rabbits found in hay.

Herbivore Rabbits are herbivores because they do not meat. Instead, they eat different kinds of greens and grains.

Hutch The name for a pet rabbit's home, which is supplied by the owner.

Litter The absorbent material used to line the floor of the rabbit's hutch so it can be warm and comfortable. Some good examples are hay, sawdust, and straw.

Molting The name of a stage when the rabbit loses the first baby coat of fur, at about four months old.

Myxomatosis A disease spread among wild rabbits through fleas. Vaccination shots are available from your veterinarian to prevent this disease.

Rabbit mix A dry mixture of crushed oats, maize (corn) and barley cereals to feed pet rabbits.

Rabbit pellets Ready-made food that comes complete with everything that pet rabbits need.

Warren A rabbits home in the wild, made of a network of tunnels and dens dug by the rabbits themselves.

Index